DESIGN IN FOCUS

Graphic DESIGN

David Wise

Wayland

Design in Focus

The Design Process
Graphic Design
Materials in Design
Design Technology

Editors: Joan Walters and Hazel Songhurst
Book Designer: Ross George

First published in 1990 by
Wayland (Publishers) Ltd
61 Western Road, Hove
East Sussex, BN3 1JD, England

British Library Cataloguing in Publication Data
Wise, David
   Graphic design.
   1. Graphic design – Manuals
   I. Title II. Series
   741.6

ISBN 1 85210 744 8

Typeset by Rachel Gibbs, Wayland (Publishers) Ltd
Printed in Italy by Rotolito Lombardo, Milan
Bound in France by A.G.M.

Contents

Introduction

Graphic design is concerned with the way we see and interpret things. It is about sharing ideas through drawing. It is easy to see how important graphic design is to an artist painting a picture, or a construction engineer planning a bridge. It is harder to see the importance of graphic design in our own lives. We are dependent on graphic design to inform and direct us. When we use a map, the graphic symbols help us plan our journey; at the supermarket the images on packets and tins help us find our favourite foods.

In organizing our lives, we have to make decisions to overcome problems. Designing a solution to a problem involves two activities: thinking and doing. With an understanding of graphic design, drawing may be the first step towards developing thoughts into practical actions.

Drawing is an integral part of the design process. The design process is a logical approach to dealing with problems. It represents the different stages involved in designing and making. In research, planning and presentation, drawing is the most direct and effective way of communicating ideas.

We are surrounded by graphic images all of which convey some kind of message or information. The colour of a flower attracts insects which help pollinate the plant. The markings on some animals may attract a mate, hide them from view, or deter predators. The visual images in a comic book unfold a story; the label on a can shows what is inside, whether baked beans, pet food or, perhaps, poison. Road signs direct and warn us, and maps and diagrams enable us to find our way.

Graphic design performs many important functions and, for it to be used fully, learning to communicate visually is important. Some of the earliest drawings can be seen on the walls of caves. It was not until the sixteenth century however, that drawing became established as an art-form of great importance.

Below *Fashion designers use graphic techniques to make designs for clothes more exciting.*

Left *The lines of a Mondrian painting have influenced the design of these shoes.*

It was an age when the human race was making scientific discoveries about itself and the world in which it lived. Drawing became accepted as an aid to this research as well as a creative activity on its own.

Artists and architects used drawing as a first stage in realizing their ideas. Understanding perspectives enabled them to present their ideas for the future and produce a more accurate record of the way things were during their lifetime. In an age of discovery drawing became a means of sharing, understanding and exploring new thoughts.

Graphics reflect the mood of the time. In times of peace and wealth graphics are used to decorate our environment. In times of unrest or war they are used in propaganda to summon support. In times of fast growth and great scientific development, graphics have been used to solve and present solutions to problems. Through drawing, scientists and engineers communicate their ideas.

Today, drawing is at the heart of every design activity. The human race has come a long way from scratching out primitive rock drawings: we can now draw with light on a television screen via a computer. However, our reasons for drawing remain much the same, that is to express an idea or to share a vision.

Above *The graphic design of a book cover may attract our attention and encourage us to buy it.*

Above *The shape of a high-performance motor car is carefully considered to make the car more efficient and attractive.*

Left *The outline shape of this kettle has been designed to look modern. It is unlikely to make it more efficient.*

5

The Visual Elements

WAYS OF SEEING

*Above and **top right** Nature provides us with an abundance of beautiful things – leaves, stones, wet sand, flowers – that excite the senses. Our ability to hear, touch, see, taste and smell helps us to understand and enjoy our experiences.*

We are surrounded by a multitude of shapes and forms created by nature or by ourselves. Our understanding of the world is based on our ability to recognize and identify these objects. We use all our senses to do this, as sight alone cannot give us a complete picture. Babies reach out to touch objects, taste them, react to the smell and listen for any sounds. By combining all our senses we learn to 'see'. If we lose a sense, it becomes harder to recognize and identify things.

Try some experiments with the help of some friends to discover what it is like to lose one or more of your senses. Find a soft bag (a carrier bag will do), and put a number of different objects inside it, some soft, some hard. Choose some familiar things, like an apple or an electrical plug, and some which are more unfamiliar, like a small soft toy or a strange-shaped stone. It is important to have a good mixture of objects. Ask a friend to shut his or her eyes and put a hand into the bag. Using touch alone, see how many things can be identified. Get them to describe each object in detail. Which are they unable to describe? Why are some objects easy to identify and others so hard?

We can experiment with our senses in many other ways. See if your friends can identify different smells. Place small quantities of coffee, honey, bath-salts, soap-powder, grass cuttings and any other familiar-smelling materials, in separate plastic cups. Tape card over the top of each cup so that you cannot see the contents. Make holes in the card so that your friends may

smell the scent from each cup. Get them to identify the contents. Try mixing materials together to create new scents.

If you have a tape-recorder, try recording some familiar and some strange sounds. A door opening, a tap dripping, or a clock ticking are all familiar sounds. Try to create new sounds which are not so easy to recognize.

There are many ways of 'seeing'. Someone blind from birth learns how to identify and recognize things by developing their other senses, especially the senses of touch and hearing.

Below *Sealed within glass jars, these objects would be a mystery to a blind person. In a visual world the ability to see is extremely important in helping us to identify and understand things.*

WHAT IS DRAWING?

Drawing is about making marks on a surface. It can be making marks with a pencil on a piece of paper, it can be carving lines with a piece of flint on a cave wall, or it can be dragging your toe over the sand at the beach. Drawing is also a means of expressing thoughts and communicating with others.

Humans have always felt the urge to draw. From 20,000 – 15,000 BC, primitive humans expressed themselves with drawings on rocks. These showed animals, hunters with bows and arrows, and warriors with spears.

Below The designers of this ancient Egyptian tomb hoped the animals shown in the wallpaintings would provide comfort for their dead King on his journey in the after-life.

Above This picture of a bison, painted on the wall of a cave in Spain thousands of years ago, represents a primitive artist's view of the animal.

Above *A fifteenth century painting showing an artist's vision of a saint.*

Right *Christopher Wren's plans for St. Paul's Cathedral gave a clear and detailed picture of what a part of the building would look like when it was completed.*

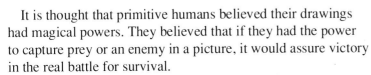

Through drawing, Michelangelo gained an understanding of the things he observed.

It is thought that primitive humans believed their drawings had magical powers. They believed that if they had the power to capture prey or an enemy in a picture, it would assure victory in the real battle for survival.

Another example of early graphics can be seen in the tombs of Egyptian pharaohs. The pyramids were built about 4,000 years ago. The inside walls were often adorned with drawings which show the paradise waiting for the dead king in his life after death.

For many religions, drawing has been a way of conveying beliefs. For 2,000 years artists have been producing images of Christ to help promote the Christian faith.

Drawing is the starting-point for all kinds of designs from kettles to cars. A design may start with simple pencil sketches and develop an idea through to detailed plans of every possible aspect to help the designer realize the idea. There are many ways of drawing, as we shall see in later chapters.

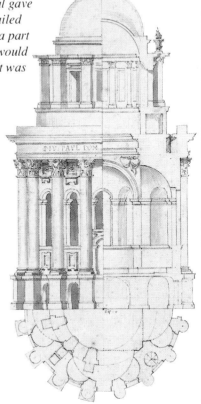

9

WHAT IS A LINE?

Take a sheet of white, A4 drawing paper. Divide the paper into four equal parts by folding it in half, then folding it in half again. Unfold the paper and you will find you have created a series of straight lines (see illustration 1). These lines may be horizontal or vertical, depending on how you divide and look at the paper.

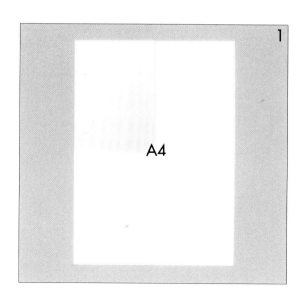

Lines suggest 'directions' because our eyes naturally follow them. A good example of directional lines can be seen on a compass. When the compass is pointing from north to south it creates a vertical line; when it points from east to west, the direction is horizontal. All other points on the compass create diagonal lines.

Any line which is not straight is curved. Quickly draw a 'straight' line without a ruler. Now draw another, this time against the edge of your ruler. Does the first line look straight or does it curve? It has been said there are no straight lines in nature. When we draw we have a natural tendency to create curving lines. Straight lines can only be achieved with drawing aids, or free-hand after a great deal of practice. Designers use lines to direct our attention and guide us along a particular route. Road signs and railway maps are often shown as a series of lines.

Start to cut into a piece of A4 white paper with a pair of scissors (see illustrations 2 and 3). Try to cut first straight, then curved lines. Keep changing direction so that you are cutting horizontal, vertical and diagonal lines. Try a variety of continuous curves and short curves. When you find you have cut from one

Above *Directional signs use lines to inform us of the direction we must take. Horizontal, vertical and diagonal lines are like arrows.*

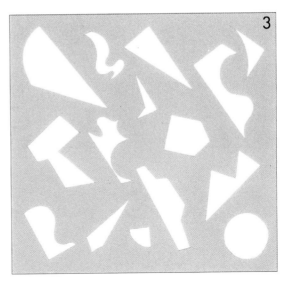

edge of the paper to the other, stop. Place the pieces of paper you have cut against a dark-coloured background. What have your cut lines produced? The A4 sheet of paper no longer exists as a simple rectangle but has become a series of smaller, more complex shapes created by the cut lines. The types of shapes you have made were decided by the direction of your lines.

Can you recognize any familiar shapes or objects in the cuts you have made? Straight cuts may have produced simple geometric shapes, like squares and triangles. Curves may have produced circles, spirals and waves. You may notice that shapes made out of straight lines tend to look like manufactured objects: houses, cars or robots. Curving shapes are more natural, suggesting animals and plants, clouds or the waves in the sea.

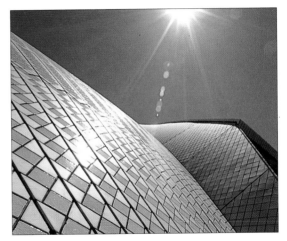

Top right *Designers use lines to create decorative patterns to make buildings, like the Syndey Opera House in Australia, more attractive.*

Right *Natural objects are often beautifully shaped and coloured which form attractive patterns like this fish photographed on a reef off Queensland, Australia.*

WHAT DO WE SEE?

When we draw, we are attempting to express a vision of something we can see or imagine. People do not always see things in the same way. What is beautiful to one person may seem ugly to another. What we actually see is the same, it is our perception, or understanding, of what we see that is different.

It is impossible for the human eye to see everything in the same detail. Our eyes can only focus on a small area within our overall field of vision. We tend to take in those things which attract our attention first; less interesting things are often ignored. Objects have visual features which act like clues to help us recognize and identify them. We see objects as a combination of visual elements. Line, shape, form, colour and texture are the main visual elements which

Careful organization of shapes and colours can produce spectacular results, like this human gymnastic display in Prague, Czechoslovakia.

come together to produce the vision of the object we see. The designer has to decide how best to use line, shape, form, colour and texture in graphic designs. These visual elements will be used to focus our attention and help us to share a common vision with the designer. To do this, the designer must take notice of certain design principles which influence how we see things. Here are the four main design principles:

- *Balance* is an important design principle. We are attracted to balance. We reject objects which are out of balance.

Right *The drawings of Escher can often deceive, and demand that we take a second look.*

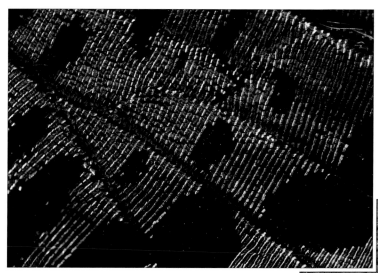

*Natural objects have surface designs which decorate or disguise. The pattern on a butterfly wing (**left**) attracts, the colour scheme of the horned frog (**below**) provides camouflage.*

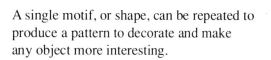

- We expect objects to be in *proportion*. If something is too big or too small it looks odd or incorrect.

- *Harmony* and *contrast* can be used to gain particular responses from people. Harmony gives a feeling of ease which is comfortable to live with; contrast creates a clash which unsettles, but attracts people's attention. All the visual elements can be used in harmonious or contrasting ways.

- *Patterns*, both natural and artificial, planned and accidental occur everywhere we look.

A single motif, or shape, can be repeated to produce a pattern to decorate and make any object more interesting.

It is the responsibility of designers to find solutions to practical problems and to create a more attractive environment. A design must work well, but it must look good too.

Graphics in Design

A designer must be able to draw. Many designers do not actually make their designs. It is very important that a designer's drawings show his or her ideas clearly and accurately to the person who is going to make the design. Through drawing, a designer shares his or her vision of how a finished product will look and how it will work.

Most professional designers have had to learn how to produce effective design drawings. They have had to learn a wide range of graphic techniques so they can communicate their ideas.

A designer will use these techniques as he or she develops an idea through the steps in the design process. Drawing will be important at every stage, from identifying the problem to testing the final solution. Simple free-hand sketches are often a starting-point, and as ideas become more definite, the drawings become more detailed. The final design drawings will show a clear picture of the designer's intentions. Perspective sketches, exploded views, colour rendering, orthographic and section drawings will show how the finished product will look, what it is made of, how it is constructed, and how it will work.

Every high-street shop is full of graphic designs. Newsagents, clothes shops, even supermarkets, sell products which have involved or contain some form of graphic image. Newspapers, magazines and book covers have all been designed to produce a visual image which will attract attention.

News-stands are full of graphic images designed to attract our attention. Good graphic design makes any newspaper and magazine worth looking at and reading.

Above left *The design on a soft drink can has to stand out against all the others on the supermarket shelves.*

Above right *Posters have always been used to inform, and warn against bad habits.*

Below *Record cover designs have become extremely important in marketing the product. Some have become collectors' items.*

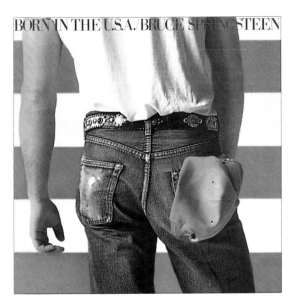

Comic books are a good example of this effect. Their brightly coloured exteriors can often be more exciting than the stories inside so that we are tempted to buy them by the cover alone.

Package design does the same job as the cover of a comic. Graphic images on the surface of a box, can, or carton make it special. The hidden contents become attractive and desirable if the package looks good. Collecting record covers has become as important as collecting the discs they protect. Postage stamps have the same appeal.

Posters are used to communicate information. They advertise everything, from what is showing at the local cinema to how to find your way around an unknown town. Billboards are a feature of nearly every city and highway. Their huge graphics encourage us to buy all kinds of goods, from a new car to a hamburger.

The manufacturer's label inside most clothes displays some kind of trademark. Some company logos are so well known that they have become international symbols. In a modern industrial society the influence of graphics in design is everywhere.

15

Graphic Techniques

TOOLS AND MATERIALS

Below *Paper is made in many sizes but the most common are graded from A1 to A6.*

Today, a huge array of graphic equipment, developed over many years of research, is available to designers. Most designs are drawn on to some kind of paper. There are many different types made from a variety of materials. Cheap papers, like newsprint, are made from wood pulp, while expensive, handmade papers are produced from linen rags. Some papers have a soft, textured surface, others are hard and smooth. Paper is available in a wide range of colours. For general design work most designers use white cartridge paper.

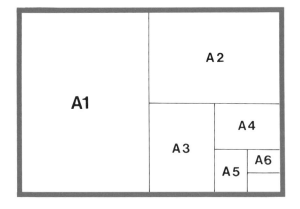

Paper can be cut to whatever size is necessary. It is produced in rolls and in single sheets. The most common sizes of paper are graded from 'A1', the largest size, to 'A6', the smallest. Each size in the sequence is half that of the previous one. Two 'A2' sheets laid side by side equal one 'A1' sheet. Designers often work on A4 and A3 design sheets.

You can make your own paper from any paper waste. The waste paper needs to be soaked in water and turned into a rich pulp which can then be poured over a flat, fine-mesh sieve to drain. The damp sheet is then pressed between two sheets of absorbent material. When all the moisture has been removed, a new sheet of paper is left behind.

Paper can be dyed or decorated before it is used for drawing. Marbling can be achieved by dipping paper into a tray of water which has been mixed with a few drops of oil-based colours. The colours float on the surface of the water and stick to the paper.

Pencils are graded according to hardness or softness. They range from 6B (very soft) to 9H (very hard). Soft pencils leave more black graphite on the paper and produce richer, darker marks. They wear away rapidly, but are ideal for quick design sketches. Hard pencils produce sharper, finer lines. They keep their point much longer and are most useful when accurate drawings with precise measurements are required. An HB pencil is in the middle of the range and can be used for most types of drawing.

Technical pens are designed to produce lines of a constant thickness. The pen nib can be changed to produce different line widths. Designers use these pens to produce clear, accurate lines which can be printed.

Pencil crayons are a very valuable tool for the designer. They can be used to produce bold, bright colours or subtle, pale shades. Pastel colours can produce some pleasing effects, but they are harder to control and tend to smudge. Felt-pens and colour markers are useful for applying colour to a design drawing. Water-based ink-markers come in a range of bright colours, but are slow to dry. Professional designers use more expensive spirit-based markers which allow them to work quickly. These are made in a carefully graded range of colours which enable the designer to produce very effective presentation drawings.

Water-based paints and inks applied with a brush or sponge can produce a variety of effects and are excellent for suggesting shape and form. Water-colours and inks are usually applied as transparent colour washes. Gouache and poster colours are more opaque because they have white added to them. They are useful for painting areas of flat, even colour or for working over other colours. The only way to achieve the best results from these graphic tools and materials is by experimenting with them.

It is important to choose appropriate tools and materials for specific design work. This will produce the best results.

FREE-HAND DRAWING

A small child first starts to draw with whatever is at hand, making marks on any surface that is available. It may be making finger lines in condensation on a window or drawing with lipstick on a wall.

In design, free-hand drawing means working without graphic aids and devices. It is a vital skill which every designer has to learn in order to realize ideas quickly in graphic form. It is said that one good drawing is worth a thousand words: a good drawing will show straight away what something will look like and is often easier to understand than a written description. Free-hand drawing is a good way to communicate ideas to others in an interesting way.

Good control in guiding the pencil over the paper is important. The pencil must draw the line you want and only practice will give you control. Good drawing also comes from careful observation. It is essential to understand the lines and shapes of what you want to draw if you are to represent it accurately. You can only learn to draw things by 'looking' at them in the right way.

Above *An artist at work in Florence, Italy.*

Below *A child paints a wall in Brixton, London.*

Try these exercises to improve your free-hand drawing skills. Choose a medium or soft pencil and work on a large sheet of white paper.

1. Draw a series of horizontal lines at least 10 cm long. Draw the first line parallel to the edge of the paper, then draw the others parallel to the first, about 1 cm apart. Work quickly, but try to keep the lines straight.

2. Do the same again, now drawing vertical lines. Do not move the paper.

3. Draw some simple shapes by crossing vertical and horizontal lines. Try to create perfect right-angles by making your lines cross at 90°. Draw a series of squares and rectangles. Inside these, try to draw some circles and ellipses.

4. Fill the rest of the paper with as many different lines as you can make: straight/curved, long and thin/short and fat, waves/zig-zags. You might like to work with other markers: pens, crayons, charcoal and paint brushes will all test your skills in producing controlled marks.

5. Try to draw an object in the room. Look closely at the object for the lines and shapes which will help you draw it. A realistic image can be achieved using very simple lines and shapes.

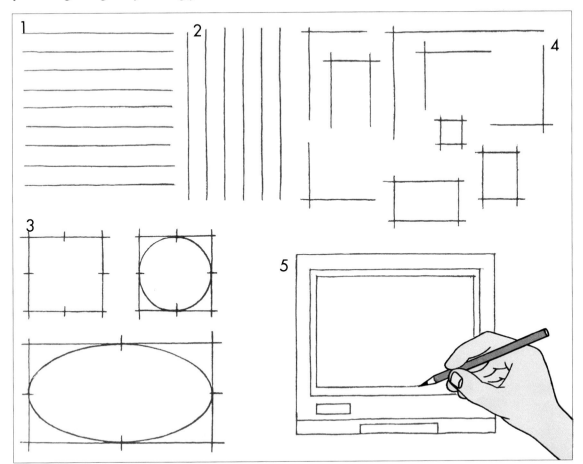

DESIGNING WITH SHAPES

Lines create shapes. When we draw lines we mark out areas on a surface. As the lines enclose these areas they become the outlines of shapes. We can describe an object simply by drawing its outline. A shape represents an object or an area which has two dimensions - length and breadth. Squares, circles and triangles are simple, geometric shapes. They are precise and can be drawn exactly. Other shapes are more difficult to describe since they tend to be based on flowing, curving lines and appear natural rather than manufactured.

Geometric shapes often make patterns which can be developed into decoration, or which can form the basic structure of an object. A square can produce a pattern which reflects the structure of a modern skyscraper, the layout of a board game (chess board), or the surface design of wrapping paper. The shapes fit together to create the design.

Nature provides an infinite number of ever-changing shapes. The structure of a plant contains many shapes which reflect patterns of growth and decay as the seasons change.

Left *The architects of the Lloyds building in London used many shapes in their design.*

Above *Shapes create patterns. Patterns can be regular or haphazard. The orderly squares of a chess board determine the movements of the pieces in the game.*

Below *You can have fun making designs based on these simple geometric shapes.*

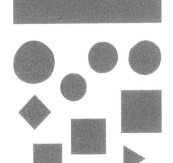

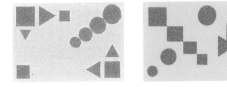

Designers have always been inspired by nature and have adapted organic shapes to their own designs.

Take a sheet of A4 coloured paper and cut out some simple geometric shapes: 4 squares, 4 circles and 4 triangles. Arrange these shapes against a different coloured background. Keep rearranging them until you find a combination you like. You may have produced an interesting pattern or created a picture of something. The outcome does not matter, what is important is that you have started to design with shapes. Shapes are the starting-point for design ideas.

Designers often use geometric shapes in their designs because they are easy to draw and can be adapted to suit a variety of needs. Geometric shapes create patterns which can make a decorative design or the framework of a structure. They are easy to recognize. For this reason, many companies have logos or trademarks in the form of geometric shapes.

Look around your home. Can you find any designs based on geometric shapes? By looking carefully at the manufactured things in our environment, we can see how many designs have been developed from nature. Nature is reflected in objects which are round rather than square and in lines which are curved rather than straight. We can use nature's shapes to decorate our own designs. As designers or consumers, it is important to learn to recognize those shapes which will be most useful in solving design problems.

21

3-D REPRESENTATION

A flat shape often represents one side of a three-dimensional (3-D) form. 3-D objects occupy space. In trying to draw an object accurately, a designer has to show that space on the flat surface of a piece of paper.

There are many different methods of presenting 3-D forms graphically, and perhaps the simplest is oblique projection. Oblique projection is based on a flat, square-on view of an object. The flat shape is projected backwards at an angle of 45°. Try to understand this by drawing it for yourself.

Cut out a square 5 cm x 5 cm from a piece of card. Using the square as a template draw round it on a piece of paper. Reposition the card so that it is a few centimetres to the right and slightly above the original square. Draw round it again and connect the two squares by drawing diagonal lines between the corresponding corners. If you have shifted the square accurately and estimated the depth correctly you will have drawn a see-through cube. Try cutting out more complex shapes and see if you can produce their 3-D forms.

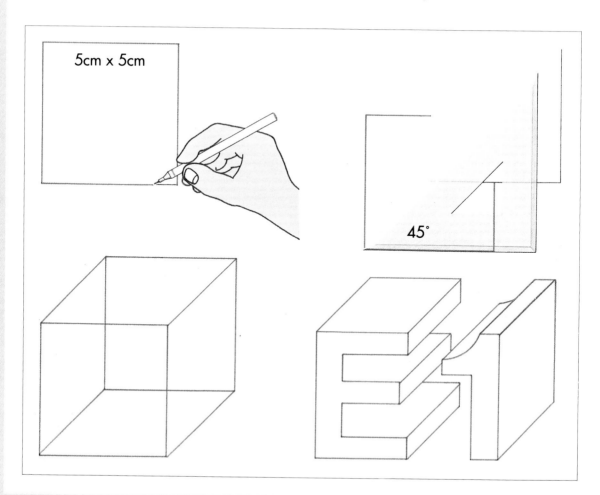

5cm x 5cm

45°

Isometric drawing is another type of three-dimensional representation. Objects are seen at an angle. All the horizontal lines in the object are angled at 30°. This type of drawing can be easily made using 30°/60° set squares, or free-hand on special isometric grid paper.

A box, like any other 3-D object, occupies a space. Drawing boxes can be used as the basis for drawing many other things. It is sometimes easier to visualize the form of an object if we can imagine what size or shape of box it will fit into. Choose an object and find a suitable viewpoint from which to draw it. Draw a box which you think represents a space the object will fit into. This box can be drawn free-hand or with the help of oblique or isometric projection. Sketch the outline of the object inside the box. You can add details later, once you are happy with the basic form of the drawing. This technique is known as crating and can be used to draw quite difficult forms.

isometric drawing 30°

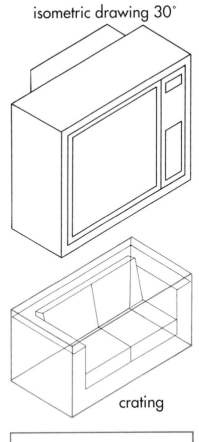

crating

60° planometric view

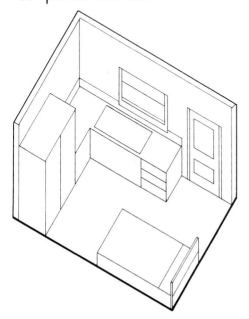

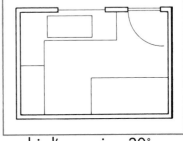

bird's eye view 30°

Another form of 3-D representation is based on what is called a planometric view. This is used to describe buildings or room interiors, working from a flat ground plan of the area to be shown. The ground plan is turned, until it is angled 45°/ 90° or 30°/60° to the horizontal. This type of drawing gives the viewer a bird's-eye view of an object or an area. Draw a plan of your bedroom and then try to produce a planometric view.

23

DRAWING IN PERSPECTIVE

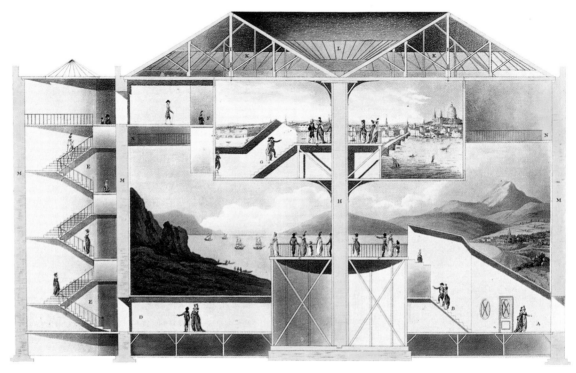

Perspective drawing involves drawing objects as you really see them. As you look around, you see objects in relationship to yourself. Your perspective will change as you change your position or viewpoint. Sitting down or standing up gives us different viewpoints and offers different perspectives.

We see objects in relationship to one another. Some objects appear close, while others seem further away. You will notice that the further away an object is, the smaller it appears. Try a simple experiment to prove this. Hold up both your hands at eye-level, about 30 cm away from your face. Move one

Perspective drawing techniques enable the designer to represent objects as we really see them.

hand a further 20 cm away. Does one hand appear to be bigger than the other? Close one eye. The difference should now become clear.

Because your viewpoint is constantly changing, drawing objects in perspective is difficult. Artists discovered a means of drawing realistic forms by looking at objects through a glass screen from a fixed viewpoint. This device, known as a Picture Obscurer, created an unchanging perspective.

The artist could draw the outline of the object on to the transparent screen and produce a more realistic picture. The shape, although drawn on to a flat, two-dimensional surface, would create the illusion of a three-dimensional form.

The two most important elements of perspective drawing are the horizon line and the **vanishing point**. On a clear, sunny day looking out to sea you are confronted by a view of the edge of the world - the line where the sky meets the sea. This edge creates a horizontal line which runs from left to right across our field of vision. It represents the point beyond which things disappear from view. Inland, the horizon is not always so obvious, obscured from view by buildings, hills and trees. However, it still affects the way we see things, because it corresponds with our viewpoint and changes according to our position. We may not always be able to see the horizon, but we can see the relationship it has with everything around us.

Standing by a railway track, looking at the rails running off into the distance gives a clear impression of how perspective works. Objects alongside the track seem to get smaller the further away they are. The gap between the rails seems to narrow until the two lines become one, just as they disappear over the horizon. From this viewpoint, by the side of the track, everything seems to meet on this one point - the vanishing point. In perspective drawings, the positions of the horizon line and the vanishing point determine the way others understand our drawings.

The point on the horizon where lines seem to converge is called the vanishing point.

ONE- AND TWO-POINT PERSPECTIVE

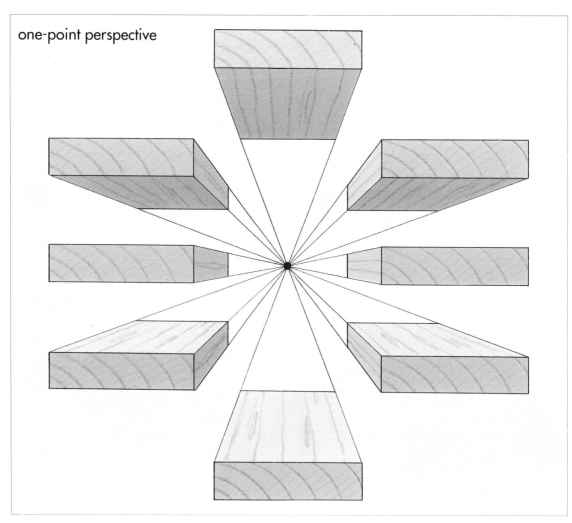

one-point perspective

One-point perspective is the simplest form of perspective drawing. Lines are drawn from points around a flat shape to meet at a single vanishing point. Along the receding lines, points can be plotted which show the depth of the object. It is possible to measure the width and breadth of the flat shape accurately, but its depth has to be estimated. A drawing produced in this way shows a three-dimensional form receding into the distance. The position of the vanishing point decides the view you create of the object.

Two-point perspective is a way of drawing objects which are not square-on to the viewer. When the object is at an angle, two sides can be shown, receding towards two vanishing points set on the horizon line. You can achieve a different view of an object by drawing it above or below the horizon or to the left or the right of the page. The distance between the vanishing points is important. If they are too close together an object looks small and distorted. Setting them far apart makes objects look larger. Vanishing points and horizon lines can be imaginary, that is, set off the paper to create different perspectives and large-scale drawings.

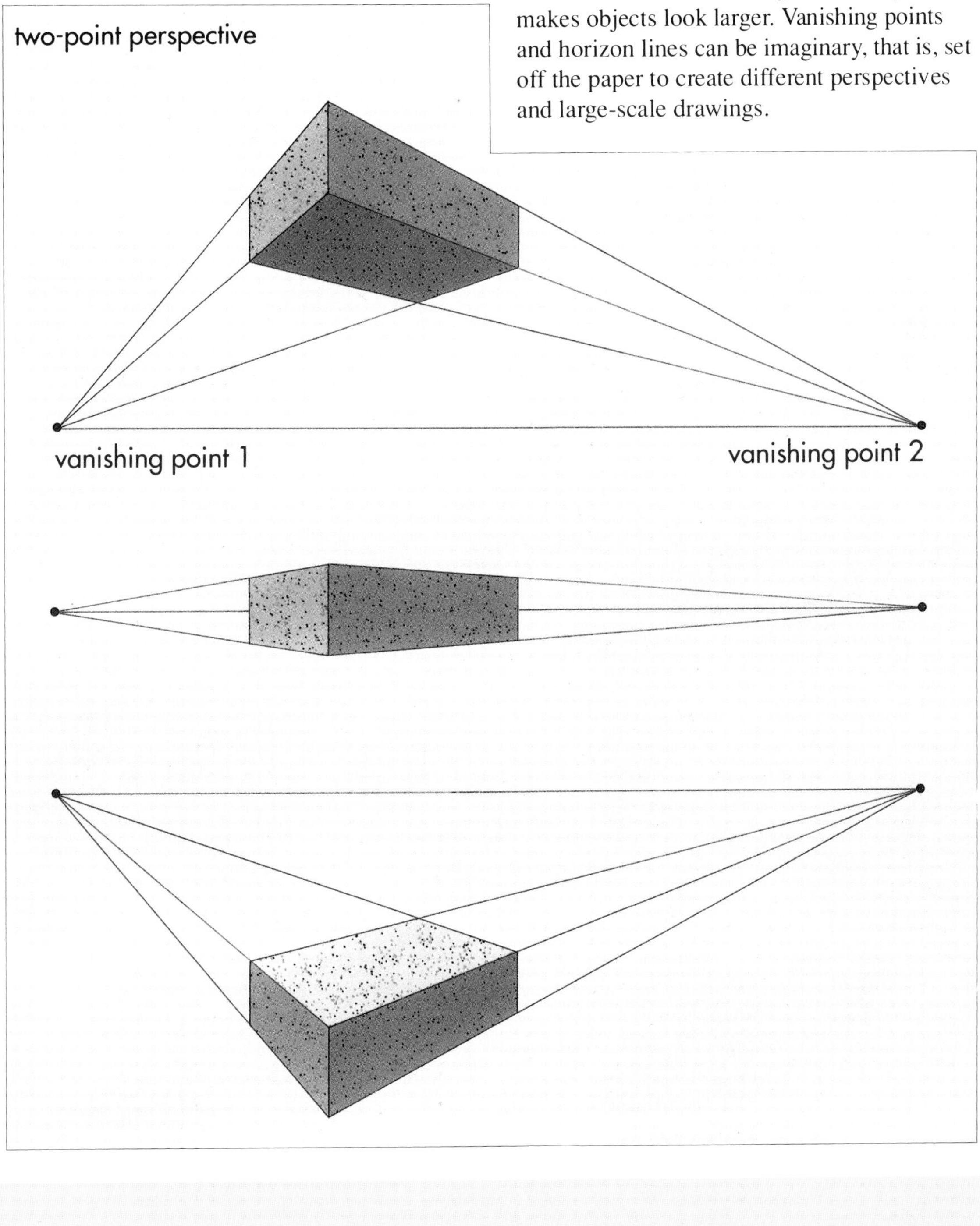

two-point perspective

vanishing point 1

vanishing point 2

WORKING DRAWINGS

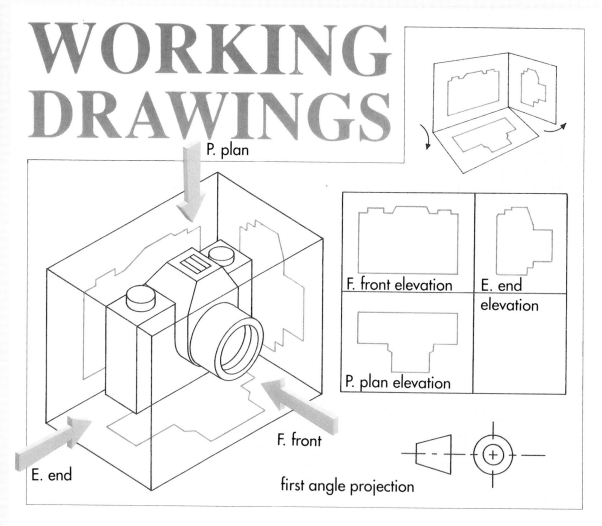

P. plan

F. front elevation

E. end elevation

P. plan elevation

F. front

E. end

first angle projection

Once a designer arrives at a solution to a design problem, he or she has to produce working drawings. Working drawings contain all the information needed to make ideas real. They show how an object will look, all its components and dimensions and how it will be made.

Three flat views, or plan elevations, are drawn, showing the front, the side and top. This type of drawing is called orthographic projection. There are two types of orthographic projection; first angle and third angle. There is little difference between the two. Both are based on the idea of looking at an object suspended in a box. The three

views, or elevations, are projected on to the surface of the box. When the box is unfolded, the three elevations are seen side by side on the same surface, or plane.

Orthographic projection shows things in great detail. It should contain all the information required for another person, apart from the designer, to realize the design. If a design needs to be made from several parts, it may be useful to show this in a working drawing. We can describe how something is put together by producing an exploded view. The component parts of the object are shown set out in the order in which they will fit together.

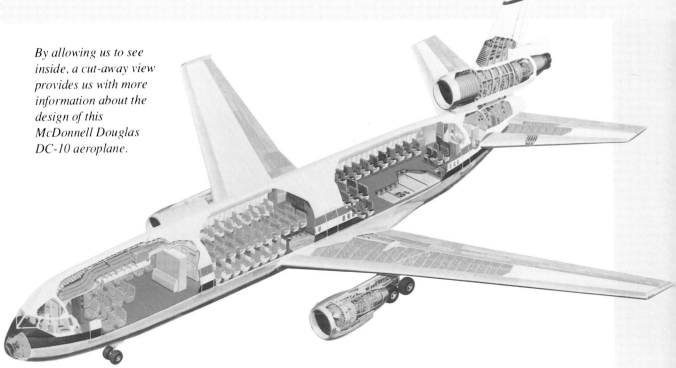

By allowing us to see inside, a cut-away view provides us with more information about the design of this McDonnell Douglas DC-10 aeroplane.

Sometimes, the inside of an object may need to be shown clearly and this can be achieved with a section drawing. A sectional view shows the object as if it had been cut in half. A cut-away view may show part of the inside of the object by taking off part of the outside covering. Designers often use this technique to show features normally hidden like the engine, suspension, or steering system on a car.

A particular technique or procedure can be called a working drawing. Flow or sequence diagrams use drawings to show different stages of an operation. Much modern furniture comes packed flat in a box. Flow diagrams show how to put it together.

Make a flow diagram to describe the sequence you follow in the morning, from the time you get up until the time you go out.

This exploded view shows how to assemble a model airplane.

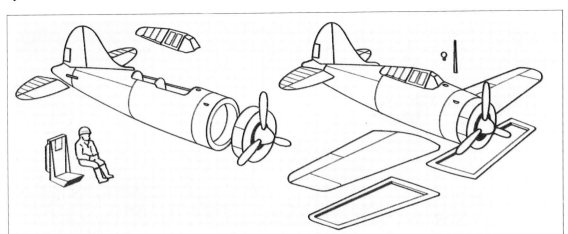

DESIGNING WITH MACHINES

Airbrushes are used in most design studios. They enable designers to work quickly to produce realistic and professional colour images. Airbrushes work by mixing air under pressure with liquid colour, paint or ink, to produce a fine spray. Compressed air, supplied from an aerosol can or electric compressor, is passed via a tube to the airbrush. The airbrush has a control valve which regulates the flow of the air-and-colour mix. With careful control, a wide range of effects can be achieved, from broad flat areas of tone to fine-detail lines.

The spread of the spray is harder to control and masking techniques are often used. Removable masking tape, or card and paper stencils, are fixed to the paper to protect certain areas from the spray. Masking fluids and masking film are more effective, but expensive alternatives.

You can produce spray-effects without an airbrush. A toothbrush dipped in paint can be used to create a splatter effect: by pulling the blade of a knife through the bristles, the colour is flicked on to the paper. A diffuser spray is two thin, plastic or metal tubes fixed together and set at right angles. One end of a tube is put into the colour and you blow down the other end. The resulting air/colour mix creates a spray effect.

*To use an airbrush effectively (**below**) demands considerable skill. Drawings produced by an expert (**right**) are often so realistic they might be mistaken for photographs.*

The computer is now a vital tool in the range of modern graphic equipment. It works from a precise programme. This tells the computer how to work by giving it a logical order in which to perform certain tasks. Information is fed into it via a mouse, a light pen or keyboard, by audio-cassette or disk drive, and images are generated on a monitor or Visual Display Unit (VDU).

The computer is able to store large amounts of information. This facility can be of great use when designing solutions to complex problems. Teams of designers, investigating different aspects of a problem, can store the results of their research in the computer. The information can then be organized and made available whenever it is needed.

The computer can be programmed to perform complex tasks. A simple two-dimensional image can be put up on the screen, extended, and shown in its 3-D form. It can then be rotated, so that it is seen from every angle. The development of computer graphics has reached the stage where computer-generated images cannot be distinguished from photographs. Many of the graphics you see at the beginning and end of television programmes have been produced by computers.

Computer Aided Design (CAD) plays an increasingly important role in the design of many manufactured goods. The design of most modern cars will have been developed with the help of CAD.

Computers have taken graphic design into a new dimension and have become an invaluable resource for many modern designers.

Design and Communication

PRESENTING THE IDEA

To develop a design idea into a realized form, a designer must usually look for expert help and advice. For example, a designer may not be able to make his or her designs, but can still present ideas as to how they may be made or what they will look like. Good presentation will attract a manufacturer who will realize the designer's ideas by providing money, materials and machines.

Detailed presentation of ideas has been important in design for a very long time. In the past, when a patron commissioned an artist, craftsperson or architect to create an artifact to his or her specifications, the designer was expected first to produce drawings and models of the end product. The same procedure still exists. Designers must gain the confidence of their customers and they gain this support only by presenting a convincing case that shows their ideas to be viable and likely to succeed.

Presenting design ideas demands many skills: realistic drawings, working models, clear, written descriptions outlining methods and procedures, all help present an idea clearly. Before artists discovered the means to draw things in 3-D they represented all objects as flat shapes. True presentation drawings were first made when perspective drawing began, about four hundred years ago.

Ideas for a new product must be well presented to attract a manufacturer.

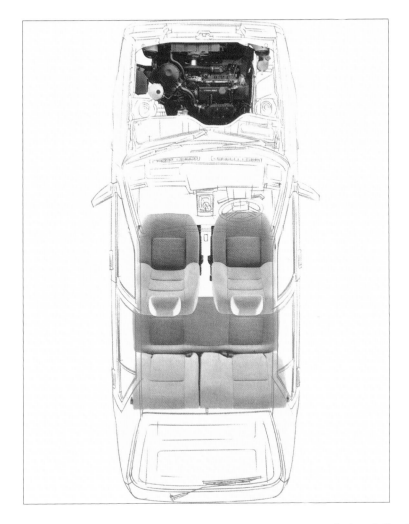

Part of an advertisement for a new car showing the interior and the engine. The designer has used a combination of graphic skills and photography to present the car to the public.

An understanding of perspective enabled artists to draw things as they really saw them and designers were able to produce a realistic impression of what they intended to make. These new skills in draughtsmanship were developed mainly in architectural drawings. The people who commissioned new buildings expected to see a clear picture of what their money was going to buy.

Many magnificent architectural designs exist as drawings only, since they failed to satisfy whoever commissioned them. A huge number of professional designs reach presentation stage and progress no further.

Designing is a very competitive activity in an industrialized society and market forces decide which designs are developed. The 'look' of a new car is extremely important. Designers know that if the customer is not attracted by the appearance of the car, he or she is unlikely to buy it. Car manufacturers are constantly developing new styles in preparation for future markets. Considerable time is spent on research into trends, and presentation drawings are produced to help visualize these predictions.

Developing ideas first as drawings and models saves money, since developing unresearched designs could produce something that nobody wants.

PRESENTATION TECHNIQUES

Presentation drawings are well organized, high-quality pieces of graphic design. Every aspect of the presentation is considered. The design will be presented as a perspective colour drawing and a variety of rendering techniques will be used to suggest the surface appearance of the object.

Pencil crayons are useful for developing tones and can create strong, textured effects.

Below *A wide range of graphic tools and materials are available to help the designer produce high-quality presentation drawings.*

Pastels work well on coloured paper and give the effect of shiny or transparent materials. Marker pens are excellent for representing plastic and metal surfaces. Paints and inks can be used for highlights and shadows as well as interesting backgrounds. The designer uses contrasting effects to focus the viewers attention on the object.

Lettering is important and is used on presentation drawings. Handwritten lettering can be very attractive, but needs to be clear. Lettering can be stencilled for neat results, but this sometimes looks dull. Transfer lettering is widely used for professional presentation drawings.

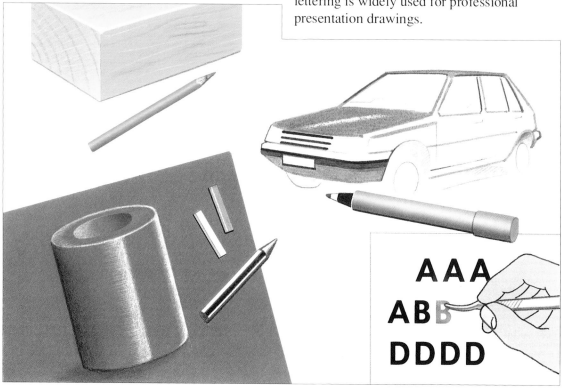

Model-making is another way to present an idea. Presentation models are perfect, scaled-down imitations of the finished product. They help the designer to show his or her client what the design will look like when it has been made. Models can be built in a range of sizes from a variety of materials. They are often made to test an idea before the final design is realized. Full-scale models are used to test a design for its efficiency in real conditions. Clay models of car bodies are built full-scale and tested in wind tunnels to find out how their shape reacts to different weather conditions.

Small-scale models give an idea of what the real object will look like and how it can be built. Architects and furniture designers often use small-scale models. Large-scale models are used to show the workings of small products. If a product is very small, such as a micro-switch, it is sometimes difficult to recognize potential problems. Large-scale models make research easier.

Working models are useful to demonstrate how something will work or behave. Construction kits are often used for this type of model. Even the simplest model, made from paper, card and string will be valuable in developing and presenting a design idea.

Top right *Presentation drawings must be accurate. The final design should present a clear picture of what the finished product will look like. This draughtsman is designing hi-fi equipment.*

Right *Architects and civil engineers use scale models to help them visualize their ideas when planning new environments for our towns and cities.*

35

DESIGN AND COMMUNICATION IN SOCIETY

Design and communication are active in every human environment. Every home contains a wealth of designed products. Package designs have an influence on what we buy, including food and groceries. The graphic symbols on the washing machine tell us how to use it. Labels inside clothes give information, including washing instructions, where they were made and from what materials. Route maps and timetables make travelling by bus or train easier. Road signs direct and warn car drivers on busy roads, and inside the car are more graphic symbols and signs. These tell the driver when fuel is running low, levels of oil and water, how to change gear, and so on.

Good design and communication means that schools, offices and factories can run smoothly. Most forms of entertainment rely on some form of graphic design to guide and inform. In the theatre and cinema, on television, in magazines and newspapers graphic images are used to communicate information. In sport, the number or letter on a player's shirt shows his or her position of play during the game. A soccer pitch or tennis

The labels in our clothes tell us where the item of clothing was made, what it is made from and how best to wash and iron it.

There are many graphic signs in our environment that direct and inform us but none so eye-catching as neon advertisements.

court is divided into areas by lines and grids. Television, perhaps the most popular form of entertainment, is one of the most powerful mediums for design and communication.

Design is an important feature in every society. Graphic design is an integral part of the design process and every designer needs to learn good graphic skills in order to communicate ideas.

Graphic designers confront our visual senses with line, shape, form, colour and pattern in an attempt to guide and inform us. Our environment is full of visual signs and symbols created by designers. They attract our attention and present us with images that are often difficult to forget.

Architects create in their drawings an image of what a building will look like before building has begun. They present us with a vision of the future. Advertisers produce designs which they wish us to believe reflect what is popular and desirable today. Artists often try to present us with a picture of what was, what is and what may yet be. For all artists and designers drawing is a means of communicating ideas. It is a way of getting the message across. The graphic work they produce contributes to the visual appearance of the world. It can influence the way we see things by directing our attention and making us focus on things we may not have noticed before. In affecting the way we see, it can also influence the way we think and act.

Graphic design is like an international language and drawing remains, as it was for those Stone Age inhabitants of caves, the most direct means we have of communicating with one another.

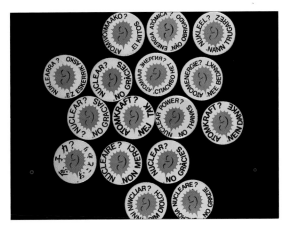

Left *'Nuclear Power? No thanks!' badges are issued in many languages by Friends of the Earth.*

Below *These graphic symbols direct shoppers to different kinds of food in a French supermarket.*

PROJECT 1

The Need

World population is increasing steadily. New medicines and better food mean that more people survive and live longer. However, this has created new problems, such as housing shortages. In small countries with large populations there is not enough land for building. There may also be a limited supply of traditional building materials. It is the responsibility of architects, scientists and civil engineers to solve this problem.

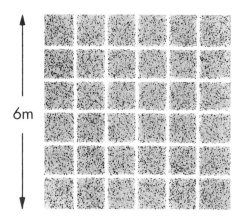

6m

free-hand sketch

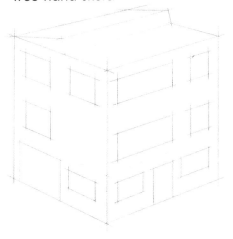

Design Brief

Design a house to suit a family of two adults and two children living in a busy, modern city. Any material can be used, but the building is limited to a ground site of 6 sq m.

Use some of the graphic techniques you have read about in this book to develop your solutions to this problem. Start by imagining the space the house will occupy. It is like a box. Do a free-hand sketch. Attempt a two-point perspective drawing when you have decided on the form your house will take. Render your drawing to show what it is constructed of.

When you have designed the outside, produce a ground plan of the inside. Use one-point perspective to give a 3-D view of some of the rooms. Why not design the fixtures and fittings too? Design the patterns on the wallpaper and curtains. You could design everything, down to the taps on the kitchen sink. Plan carefully, one day you may need to realize your ideas.

rendered perspective drawing

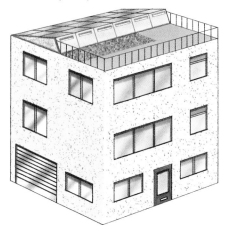

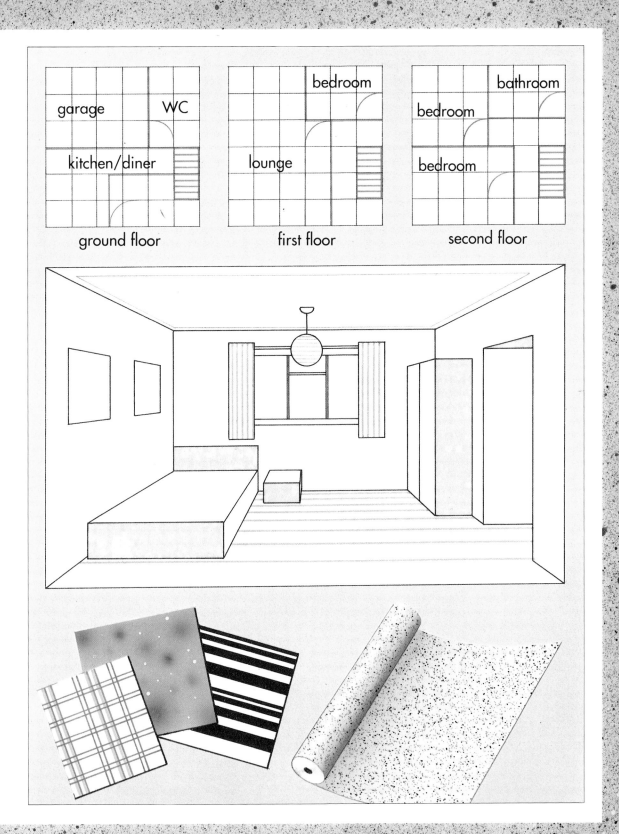

garage

WC

kitchen/diner

ground floor

bedroom

lounge

first floor

bathroom

bedroom

bedroom

second floor

PROJECT 2

The Need

Package design has become important in our lives because of the way we buy things. Most manufactured goods arrive at the shop or warehouse in some kind of package. Nearly everything comes wrapped or packaged and often the package costs more to produce than its contents.

The package designer plays a vital role in the presentation of products to the buying public, because it is his or her ideas which are first seen and which often sell the goods.

If products are not packaged attractively consumers will not be interested in buying. Using the ideas on these pages, design a package to hold an egg securely.

Design Brief

Design and construct a package to contain a chocolate easter egg.

Research

There are several points to consider. The package must support and protect the egg; the surface design should reflect what is inside; and the package construction could allow part of the egg inside to be seen.

First, you will need the egg to help you decide on the size of the package. There is no reason why a small egg cannot be contained in a big box. If you cannot buy a chocolate egg, use a hard-boiled hen's egg.

If you plan to make a box, white card will be useful, but it is important that you plan carefully and experiment with paper models first. Make a flat plan of your box, a net. This will help you construct it and will be easier to decorate in this flat form.

Look for interesting packages around the home to give you some ideas. You could use parts of some packages in your own construction. Evaluate your design by eating the egg. It should taste better!

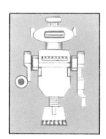

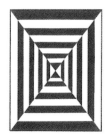

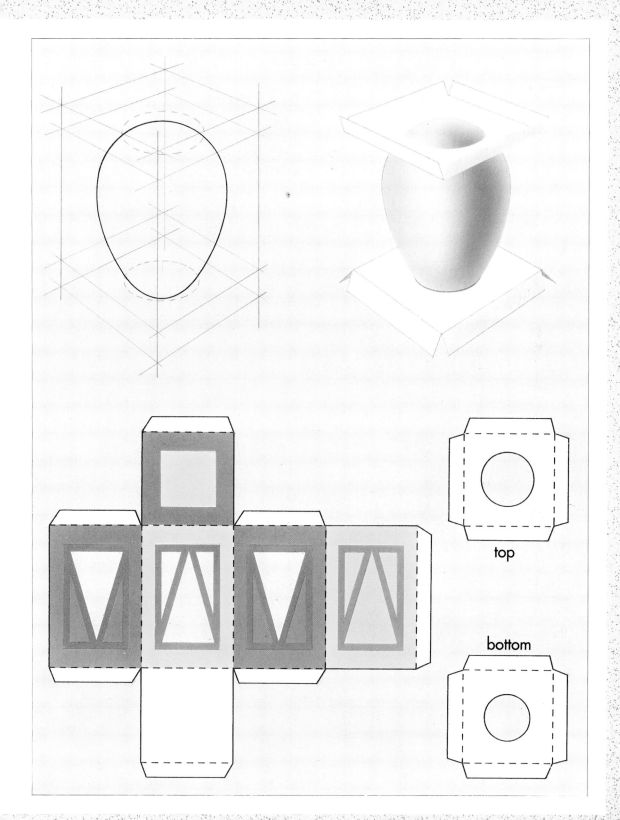

top

bottom

41

PROJECT 3

The Need

Giving presents can be expensive. As well as traditional greetings cards, you can often find more unusual kinds, including carefully engineered pieces of card sculpture. As you open the card, you are greeted by a 'pop-up' figure or message. These cards can be expensive, but are often so interesting that they make worthwhile presents.

Design Brief

Design and make an animated greetings card.

The cards below and the illustrations on page 43 may help you to create an original pop-up card.

Research

Decide on the greetings your card will present: 'Merry Christmas', 'Happy Birthday', 'Get Well Soon' or just 'Congratulations'. What form will it take? Will the part that moves represent something? You could try to design an animal that pops up and waves its arm or nods its head.

Make some sketches so that you can visualize any problems involved in making your design ideas work. Try making a few prototype models out of paper. If any work, make notes or sketches of how you made them.

Once you have solved the problem of animating the card, plan how to decorate it. What colours will suit your design and the greetings? Would you use black for a Christmas card? Design your own envelope and give the card to someone special.

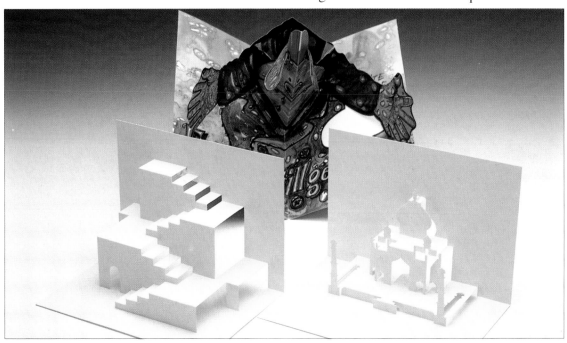

Glossary

Airbrush A drawing instrument which mixes air and colour under pressure to create a fine spray.

Animated A series of drawings which appear to move when viewed quickly one after another, such as a cartoon.

Architect A person responsible for the design of buildings and other complex structures.

Artifact An object produced through craft and design.

Artist A creative person, skilled in arts and crafts.

C.A.D. Computer Aided Design.

Consumers Users or purchasers of goods [materials/artifacts/products].

Craftsperson A skilled worker or skilful artist.

Crating A type of 3-D drawing in which the outline of the object is drawn within the framework of a transparent box.

Cut-away view A drawing which shows the features of an object that are normally hidden.

Design Process The different stages of designing and making.

Diffuser spray A drawing implement used for applying ink or paint.

Draughtsmanship The art or skill of drawing, generally plans.

Ellipse A shape that looks like a flattened circle.

Exploded view A diagram to show the assembly of all component parts of an object.

Free-hand drawing Drawing by hand without the use of drawing aids and instruments.

Geometric shapes Regular shapes with easily defined areas.

Gouache An opaque, water-based paint.

Graphic techniques Different methods of drawing.

Graphite A natural form of carbon used in the 'lead' of pencils.

Horizon line A line which represents the division between the earth or sea and the sky, or the top and bottom of the picture (eye level).

Isometric drawing 3-D drawing in which lines are parallel and do not converge to a vanishing point (Oblique projection).

Logo Graphic symbol which represents the corporate image of a company or organization.

Market forces The influence of the consumer on design and manufacture.

Masking techniques Means of protecting areas within a design from additional overlying marks or colours.

Media The means by which an idea is expressed or a message communicated, e.g. television.

Nature Everything which has not been designed and made by human beings.

Net A flat plan of a 3-D shape.

Oblique projection Drawing of a flat shape projected backwards 45° to the horizontal to produce a 3-D form (Isometric drawing).

One-point perspective The representation of an object or scene whereby all lines converge on a single vanishing point.

Orthographic projection/drawing Drawing showing three separate views of an object: front, side and top.

Patron A supporter or employer of an artist, designer, craftsperson or engineer.

Perception The way we experience things through our senses.

Perspective A way of seeing things as they really are.

Perspective sketches Drawings which describe things as they are seen in relationship to one another.

Plan elevation A drawing of an object as seen from above; a bird's-eye view.

Planometric view A 3-D image constructed from a floor plan.

Propaganda Using the media to advertise a particular belief or view of life.

Prototype The first realization of a design in its final form.

Raw materials The basic fabric from which a design will be made.

Render To decorate a drawing of an object, usually with colour, so that it looks as realistic as possible.

Section drawing A diagram to show the inside of an object.

Senses The way we experience things through sight, sound, touch, taste and smell.

Sequence diagrams A series of drawings or photographs to illustrate the different stages of an operation.

Society The organised way of life within a community.

Texture Something you can see and touch; the surface quality of an object or material.

Trademark The registered name or device used by manufacturers to identify their products.

Transfer lettering Ready-formed letters or shapes which can be applied directly on to drawings or products.

Two-point perspective The representation of an object or scene where lines converge at two vanishing points.

Vanishing point A point, or points, on the horizon used in perspective drawings where lines converge.

Visual communication The way we receive and transmit messages using our sense of sight.

Visual elements Those things which can be identified by sight, such as line, shape, form, tone, colour, texture, pattern.

Working drawings Drawings used by designers and engineers in the making of a design idea.

Further Reading

Introducing Craft Design and Technology Andrew Breckon/David Prest (Thames/Hutchinson, 1983)
CDT Foundation Course Ed. Andrew Breckon (Collins Educational 1986)
CDT: Design and Communication Ed. Andrew Breckon (Collins Educational 1988)
Design Graphics David Fair/Marilyn Kenny (Hodder and Stoughton, 1987)

Graphics Design Source Book Liz McQuiston/Barry Kitts (Macdonald Orbis, 1987)
Presentation Techniques Dick Powell (Orbis, 1985)
The Art Label Robert Opie (Simon & Schuster, 1987)

Index

The words in **bold** refer to the pictures.

Picture Acknowledgements

The pictures in this book were supplied by:
Aldus Archive 4 (right), 5 (top), 13 (top), 29, 37 (left); The Bridgeman Art Library 9 (top left), 9 (bottom); Chapel Studios 15 (bottom), 16–17, 20, 21, 36, 40, 42; E. T. Archive 15 (top), 24; Michael Holford 8 (both), 9 (top right); The Hutchison Library 6, 10, 12, 14, 35 (top); Oxford Scientific Films: S. Dalton 13 (centre), M. Fogden 13 (bottom), R. H. Kuiter (bottom right); Topham Picture Library 4 (bottom), 5 (left), 5 (centre), 7 (both), 15 (top left), 18 (bottom), 31, 35 (bottom), 37 (bottom); A. Walters 11 (top right), 30 (both); Wayland Picture Library (Julie Davey)18 (top). Artwork on cover and on pages 12–13 and 25 by Kevin Hauff. All other artwork by Martin Newton. Graphic materials for the photograph on pages 16–17 kindly supplied by *Artscene*, Bond Street, Brighton.